Gifts from the Heart

Dolley Carlson
illustrated by Kathleen O'malley

Chariot VICTOR
PUBLISHING
A DIVISION OF COOK COMMUNICATIONS

Little book
be on your way

Bless the reader's
heart I pray

Victor Books is an imprint of ChariotVictor Publishing,
a division of Cook Communications, Colorado Springs, Colorado, 80918.
Cook Communications, Paris, Ontario
Kingsway Communications, Eastbourne, England

Gifts from the Heart
© 1997 by Dolley Carlson for text

Designed and edited by Brenda Franklin
Illustrated by Kathleen O'malley

All Scripture quotations, unless indicated, are taken from the Holy Bible: New International Version©. Copyright © 1973, 1978, 1984 by International Bible Society. Used by permission of Zondervan Publishing House. All Rights Reserved.

Scripture quotations followed by NASB are taken from New American Standard Bible, © the Lockman Foundation, 1960, 1962, 1963, 1968, 1971, 1972, 1973, 1975, 1977.

Scripture quotations followed by KJV are taken from the Holy Bible, King James Version.

Scripture quotations followed by TLB are taken from The Living Bible, © 1971, Tyndale House Publishers, Wheaton, IL 60189. Used by permission.

"Pass It On," p. 64, © 1969 Kurt Kaiser, Lexicon music Incorporated.

Printed in China.

Library of Congress Cataloging in Publication Data

Carlson, Dolley.
        Gifts from the heart / by Dolley Carlson.
              p.   cm.
        ISBN 156476723x
        1. Friendship. 2. Interpersonal relations. I. Title.
    BF575/F66C   1998
    241'.6762—dc21
                                                    97-22396
                                                      CIP

To my husband, Tom,
and our daughters, Candy and Katie.
Gifts from God's heart to mine.

I love you all so much!

Every good gift
and
every perfect gift
is
from above,
and
cometh down
from
the Father.

—James 1:17 (KJV)

Contents

Introduction

As I look around our home, my eyes behold the precious and thoughtful gifts that family and friends have lovingly given me through the years. Although I cherish them all, even more dear to me are the "gifts from the heart"—gifts that were not only for my physical home but for my spiritual home as well . . . my heart.

Years ago my friend Diane gave me a gift from the heart when she presented me with a little cream pitcher. She said, "Dolley, every time you look at this pitcher remember that God is always pouring His blessings on you." This came at a time of great discouragement and sadness. My dear friend knew I needed to be reminded of God's constant outpouring of blessings.

Each and every new year is filled with events that call for special gifts. You can give a gift from the heart on any occasion, holiday or just 'cause. Your own heart will be richly blessed as you express God's love to others with gifts of friendship, affirmation, celebration, comfort, forgiveness, honor, hope, love, mercy, prayer, rejoicing, and tradition.

Many of the gift ideas in this little book are mine, but even more are the result of love I have seen expressed by others in a variety of creative, practical and inspirational ways. Gifts so dear, so sweet, so thoughtful, they are never forgotten.

I've written this book as a tribute to the Lord. His loving presence in our hearts miraculously transforms us from mere mortals to vessels of His love. In Jesus, the possibilities are endless, and will last from here to Eternity. Gifts from the heart are like that . . . they keep on giving and giving.

Friendship

The gift of **friendship**—both given and received—is joy, love and nurturing for the heart. The realization that you have met a soul mate . . . a kindred spirit . . . a sister . . . a true friend . . . is one of life's **sweetest** gifts!

a friend loves at all times.—Proverbs 17:17

Friends Share the Sorrow & Divide the Joy!

The Bible is rich with examples of dear friends and how they blessed each other. For example, mary and Elizabeth had the excitement of being pregnant at the same time. **JOY!** Ruth and naomi were not only mother and daughter-in-law but also good friends who both became widowed. The sorrow they shared provides us with a loving example of loyalty, caring and hope.

my friend is not perfect, nor am I, we suit each other perfectly!

Honesty Is Best

When you're transparent it frees friends to share, and your hearts will meet at the intersection of love and support.

Show You're Interested

What's going on in your friend's life? How's your friend's heart? What are her struggles? Don't forget to ask!

Give Her Space

One woman who has many friends said, "You gravitate toward people who don't have expectations of you."

Be Trustworthy

Hold in confidence any details of your friend's business, and **keep secrets** just that—a secret!

 27 Wonderful
to Show Your

1. Call just to say "Hi!" (be careful not to call only with business or to ask for a favor).

    2. Plan a fun "out-of-the-ordinary" outing.

3. Give or send flowers—just 'cause!

    4. Love her family.

        5. Send an anniversary card with a note to her parents.

        6. Provide dinner when she's sick or after the arrival of a new baby.

7. Offer to help her with an overwhelming project.

        8. Give small presents to her children on their special occasions or to celebrate accomplishments.

9. Surprise her on the morning of her birthday with cinnamon rolls, a candle, confetti, and streamers.

    10. Clean her house when she's sick.

11. Send a note affirming her as a wife, mother or friend.

        12. Present her with a gift certificate for a pedicure in her 4th month of pregnancy.

    13. Compliment her—often and with sincerity.

    14. Pray regularly for her and her loved ones.

 8

& Loving Ways
Friend you Care

15. Organize contributions from several couples to foot the bill for a night away when she and her husband have been under a lot of stress.

    16. Give her space.

        17. Send her a Scripture verse in a pretty card or leave one on her answering machine.

        18. Be available.

        19. Offer forgiveness.

20. Extend to her unconditional acceptance.

      21. Make an acrostic with her name:

G iving
A vailable
I ntelligent
L oving

22. Give her a snapshot of the two of you or the bunch of you.

    23. Surprise her with a pretty ribbon or clip for her hair.

    24. Throw her an encouragement luncheon (just like a birthday party) to help her through a difficult time.

25. For a fun Autumn gift, put a pumpkin, bottle of apple cider and popcorn in a box, drop it on her doorstep, ring the bell, and run.

26. Plan a picnic after church for your families.

27. Give her your trust.

Dear Friend

When two fond hearts
    become dear friends
        The joy and blessings
           never end.
  When two fond hearts
      can pray together
        They never have to
           wonder ever,
If Jesus hears
    their pleas and praise,
        As they seek to imitate
          His ways.
           When two fond hearts . . .

The inspiration for this poem came from meeting with my friend Gail every other Tuesday morning for breakfast, sharing God's word, counsel, prayer, tears, and laughter. I gave it to her as a birthday gift from the heart.

When you make friendships a priority, God blesses your effort. Remember, if you aim at nothing, you'll hit it every time. Teri and I have been friends for almost 26 years. Our lives have always been very busy with raising families, serving in ministry, homemaking, and work. However, we have always made our friendship a priority, carving out little bits of time to catch up on each other's lives. We often do this over a cup of steaming hot tea and a little something sweet. The result? A not-too-fussy but still-very-pretty tea party for two!

I am delighted to share my Banana Good-for-You Cake recipe. It's Teri's favorite. The making and baking is a gift from the heart.

Banana Good-for-you Cake

1/2 cup butter or margarine
1 cup light brown sugar
1/2 cup granulated sugar
2 eggs
1 tsp. grated lemon peel
1 1/4 cups sifted flour
1/2 tsp. salt

1/2 tsp. baking powder
3/4 tsp. baking soda
1/3 cup buttermilk
3/4 cup oatmeal
1 cup mashed bananas
3/4 cup raisins

Cream together butter and sugars. Add eggs and lemon peel. Beat well. Sift together flour, soda, baking powder and salt. Add dry ingredients alternately with buttermilk to creamed mixture. Stir in oatmeal with banana and raisins. Pour batter into 2 greased and floured 8" baking pans. Bake at 350 degrees for 25 to 30 minutes. Cool completely on wire cake racks. Frost with cream cheese frosting.

Cream Cheese Frosting

1 8 oz. package cream cheese, softened
1 3/4 cups powdered sugar
2 tbs. lemon juice
1 tsp. grated lemon peel
A sprinkling of finely crushed nuts of your preference

Combine cream cheese, sugar, lemon juice and lemon peel. Blend until smooth (add a little more lemon juice if too thick). Frost between cake layers and top of cake, letting frosting drip down sides rather than frosting completely. Sprinkle a small amount of finely grated lemon peel and finely chopped nuts on cake top. Enjoy!

'Stay' is a charming word in a friend's vocabulary.—Louisa May Alcott

If you're lonely for friends—take it to Jesus.
    If you're struggling with a present friendship—take it to Jesus.
If your heart is full of thankfulness for your friends—thank Jesus.
    And most of all, remember that the best friend you or I
        will ever have is JESUS!

affirmation

I thank my God every time I remember you. In all my prayers for all of you, I always pray with joy because of your partnership in the gospel from the first day until now, being confident of this, that He who began a good work in you will carry it on to completion until the day of Christ Jesus.—Philippians 1:3-6

The One-Size-Fits-All Kind of Gift!

affirmation. It's the one gift that is always in style, always in season, and always just the right size! Do you like to be affirmed? I'd be quite surprised if your answer was anything but yes. Everyone likes to be appreciated. affirmation helps to keep us going in the right direction. It's a warm reflection of how you and I bless others.

When was the last time you sat down and made a list of those people in your life who need affirmation? Sometimes the person least likely to come to mind is the person who might need it most. For example, what about your grocery store checkout clerk? You probably have a favorite one. Just imagine how good it would feel for him or her to hear, "I so appreciate you. You're always so friendly and my children love you! Thank you for being so pleasant!" Try it the next time you shop.

What about the mechanic who takes care of your car? Our mechanic is Norm. He's honest as the day is long. You can't even imagine how much we appreciate him! Not long ago, I asked Norm if he had a picture of himself at work. He said, "No." When I discovered he had been in business for 25 years, I told him, "The next time I come, I'm bringing my camera to take a picture of you and the guys!" My intent is to make it a Christmas gift. I'm doing this for my hairdresser, favorite grocery clerk, bank teller, aerobics teacher, doctor, and nurse. I'm sure the Lord will bring some other wonderful people to mind! Oops, He just did: my pastor!

12

8 Awesome Acts of Affirmation

In our relationships we need to be love finders, not fault finders.—Charles Ara

Warm Welcomes
Acknowledging someone's arrival or presence is a great way to affirm someone. Make it a point to say, "Hi! I'm glad you're here!" (And don't forget the hugs!)

Save a Seat
When you notice that your friend is running late, save her a seat. That's affirmation, grace and mercy all rolled into one!

Meet Your Mate
Does your husband need affirmation? Of course he does! Our evening is so different when I meet my husband at the door with "Hi, handsome!" rather than "Gosh, do you look tired!"

Sow Seeds of Support
Plant colorful flowers by your friend's front door while she's not home. Flowers send such loving thoughts, and it's extra fun to do it anonymously!

Become an Affirmation Angel
Leave messages (anonymously or not) of appreciation on your friend's answering machine. Her heart will be warmed when she hears a message like "You did a great job of . . ." or "Thank you for . . ."

Praise the Parents
When you meet your friend's parents, share what you appreciate about their child. The Lord gave my friend Linda the gift of loving people just as they are. So I shared with her mother, "What goodness you must have filled your little girl with. She always has so much love and patience to give to others."

Birthday Bouquet
When celebrating a birthday, affirm the guest of honor with loving statements such as "Thanks for seeing the best in us." or "You're such a good listener."
You will be creating a verbal bouquet of affirmations she can carry in her heart forever.

"Cheers for You" Chocolate
I love to make up little cellophane-wrapped dessert gifts for my friends, family and people I see along life's way. I don't know anyone who doesn't like chocolate, so I most often make my Fudge-Topped Brownies (recipe on the next page).

Fudge-Topped Brownies

1 cup butter or margarine
1/3 cup unsweetened cocoa powder
1 cup water
2 cups all-purpose flour
2 cups granulated sugar

1 tsp. baking soda
1/2 tsp. salt
2 slightly beaten eggs
1/2 c. buttermilk
2 tsp. vanilla

Combine butter, cocoa and water in saucepan. Stir constantly while bringing to a boil. Remove from heat. Combine flour, sugar, soda and salt in large mixing bowl. Stir in eggs, buttermilk and vanilla. Add cocoa mixture and mix together until blended. Pour into one greased (I use nonstick spray) 15 1/2 x 10 1/2 x 1 inch baking pan or 2 greased 9 x 9 x 2 inch baking pans. Frost with fudge frosting while still warm. Cool to room temperature before cutting.

Fudge Frosting

1 stick butter
3 rectangles of unsweetened baking chocolate
1 1/2 16 oz. boxes of powdered (confectioner's) sugar
1 1/2 tbsp. vanilla
hot water

Melt butter and chocolate over very low heat or in double boiler. Turn off heat. (I usually put the pan in the sink so the sugar and chocolate won't hit the wall or stove.) Add powdered sugar and vanilla. Mix with electric beater on low. Add very hot water a little at a time to reach desired consistency.

Consistency should be thick enough not to be drippy but thin enough to spread evenly. Cut frosted brownies into small squares. Place on pretty paper plate (dessert or luncheon size). Generously wrap with cellophane and tie with a pretty ribbon. Affirm with chocolate!

Whatever is true, whatever is noble, whatever is right, whatever is pure,
whatever is lovely, whatever is admirable—if anything is excellent
or praiseworthy—think about such things.—Philippians 4:8

Hope

Be strong and take heart, all you who hope in the Lord.
—Psalm 31:24

I have learned to have complete confidence in the Lord's plan for my life. Remembering that our final destiny is heaven puts everything here on earth in perspective. Plant God's word in your heart and watch hope grow!

When we hope in the Lord, we do not hope in vain. Romans 5:5 reminds us, "Hope does not disappoint us, because God has poured out his love into our hearts by the Holy Spirit, whom He has given us."

Always remember that there is nothing that happens to you or me that Jesus doesn't know about. Jeremiah 29:11 states that He is our hope always: "'For I know the plans I have for you,' declares the Lord, 'plans to prosper you and not to harm you, plans to give you hope and a future.'"

Trouble is part of your life, and if you don't share it, you don't give the person who loves you a chance to love you enough.—Dinah Shore

When You Are Without Hope

Look up the word "hope" in the concordance of your Bible and do a word study.

The Lord is good to those whose hope is in Him, to the one who seeks Him.
—Lamentations 3:25

When a Friend Is Without Hope

She will need you to bridge the gap between discouragement and hope with prayer and action. It's easy to become paralyzed by hopelessness. I was in this situation several years ago and chose to isolate myself from friends and activity. One day a close friend phoned and was very sensitive to the sound of my voice. She became quite assertive and direct: "Dolley, meet me in front of your house in three minutes. I'm taking you out for Chinese food." I gave several excuses but she persisted. "Well, just meet me out front so we can visit." She pulled up, opened the car door and said, "Dolley, get in!" I did and was grateful for her perseverance. Her love and determination got me out of my paralytic state of hopelessness. I wasn't free to discuss the situation and appreciated that she didn't pry. She rescued me from my tears and troubles and helped me take the first step toward new hope.

For you have been my hope, O Sovereign Lord, my confidence since my youth.—Psalm 71:5

Empty-nest Syndrome

This can be a time of hopelessness for many women. Having dedicated herself to a job she wholeheartedly loved—that of being a mom—and then finding herself out of work at mid-life can be very discouraging. Here's a couple of ways you can help:

Let her know she is in your thoughts. Buy four pretty note cards or postcards, and write to your friend. Affirm her giftedness and talents, as well as a job well done with her children. The message need not be lengthy—short and sweet is perfect! Then, send them, one at a time, throughout the week.

Suggest that the two of you take a class together to improve existing skills or learn new ones. Midlife offers the opportunity to explore new areas of interest and service we weren't able to pursue while raising our children. Help your friend to see the second half of life as the Lord's wonderful adventure.

But those who hope in the Lord will renew their strength. They will soar on wings like eagles; they will run and not grow weary, they will walk and not be faint.—Isaiah 40:31

When a Situation Seems Hopeless

Remember that as Christians, we are never without hope. We have the Lord on our side! We need only to trust and put our hope in Him and His many promises. Don't forget that He loves you and that He knows best! His words to us in Romans 12:12 tell us to be joyful in hope, patient in affliction, faithful in prayer.

Love

Dear friends, let us love one another.—1 John 4:7

A Gift from the Heavenly Father's Heart to Ours

We all want to love and be loved. When we understand and accept the fathomless love the Lord has for us, we walk through life like loved people, loving others and trusting their love for us. And, we are able to give love freely, without reservation or fear of rejection.

♥ ♥ ♥

I have an old home movie of my father-in-law pushing a baby carriage in the fall of 1943. I think it must have been a Sunday because he is wearing a suit and sporting a very handsome hat (the kind you see in Elliot Ness movies). As David Carlson is walking toward the camera, he stops, smiles, leans into the carriage and kisses the baby. He smiles for the camera again, leans in and kisses the baby again. Then he reaches in, picks up the baby, holds him up for the camera, turns the little baby's head so you can see the little baby's face, and kisses the baby once more.

That baby was my husband, Tom, and he was greatly loved by his father. Tom walks through life like a loved person, with gentle strength, quiet confidence, a servant's heart, and a capacity to love people right where they are—even if that place is somewhat off center! He is a peaceful and joyous man.

Jesus kisses us with each and every word of the Holy Bible, embraces us with the comfort of the Holy Spirit and holds us up for the world to see—that we are His and we are loved.

How great is the love the Father has lavished on us, that we should be called children of God! And that is what we are!—1 John 3:1

Turn Thoughts into Actions

What are your thoughts? Are they of love and affection? Proverbs 23:7 says, "For as he thinks within himself, so he is" (NASB). A genuine love for others produces tangible actions. Does your hospitality, empathy, fidelity, and contentment reflect love?

Who Needs a Love Letter from You?

Plan a time alone with the Lord, and ask who He would have you write a love letter to. Review the 1 Corinthians 13 list below and see who comes to mind. Is it your spouse, roommate, mother, father, brother, sister, friend, or child? It's so easy to take the people closest to us for granted. At a women's retreat, a young mother came up to me and said she was going to write a love letter to her middle son. "Dolley, I'm always telling him 'no' and correcting him for one thing or another. I want him to know that his daddy and I really do love him." Perhaps your love letter is to Jesus? When's the last time you told Jesus how much you love Him? Think how happy you would be to receive a love letter. Now sit down and begin your letter. You'll receive blessings all around, I promise!

Love is patient,
love is kind.
It does not envy,
it does not boast,
it is not proud.
It is not rude,
it is not self-seeking,
it is not easily angered,
it keeps no record of wrongs.
Love does not delight in evil
but rejoices with the truth.
It always protects, always trusts,
always hopes, always perseveres.
Love never fails.
—1 Corinthians 13:4-8

Love Is Patient

The heart that gives patience is willing to wait. God calls us His "children," not His "adults." By His grace we're all still growing, trying to become more like Him every day. Forest Home Christian Conference Grounds has been a "home away from home" to our family for many years. I bought a needlepoint kit there. It said, "Please be patient, God isn't finished with me yet." I began stitching it about fifteen years ago as a gift for Candy; it still isn't finished and neither are we . . .

He who began a good work in you will carry it on to completion until the day of Christ Jesus.—Philippians 1:6

Love Is Kind

Oh Lord, please give me a kind and loving heart. Frequently the needs of the very young and the very old are the same. Physical needs are easy to see and meet. But it's kindness expressed through patience and love that is often needed most of all. I was running errands with my friend and her grandmother. At least five times, the grandmother said, "Can our last stop be the grocery store so I can get some milk? I have some powdered milk, but it doesn't taste as good as fresh milk. I need to pick up a few other things too. Is that okay?" Each and every time the grandmother repeated her need, my friend treated it as the first. She was so kind, responding with "Okay, Grandma. We'll be sure to stop. I won't forget."

Love Does Not Envy

Does the green monster live in your heart? Do you tend toward envy or jealousy? These traits are known to break hearts, friendships, marriages, and break up families, fellowship groups, and churches. Confess your tendency to a trusted and wise friend. Ask your friend to pray and hold you accountable. It will take the power out of the sin and bring PEACE into your heart.

Not long ago a woman told me of her tendency to be jealous and how she took the "green monster" sin before the Lord in prayer. God granted insight as she asked herself, "How will my life change because this person has something I don't?" The answer? It won't! Will your heart be green with envy or GLORIOUS with love?

Jealousy is more dangerous and cruel than anger.—Proverbs 27:4 (TLB)

Love Is Not Rude

We need to treat our family as well as we treat our friends. For the next couple of days, listen to what you say and how you say it. Ask yourself this question, "Would I talk like this, in this tone, using these words with one of my friends?"

Love Is Not Self-Seeking

If something needs to be done, lovingly do it! Give the SACRIFICE up to the Lord, and make it your gift from the heart to Him. Katie says, "Like when it's not your turn to do the dishes and you do them anyway!"

9 Expressions of Love

Birthday parties are a wonderful way to express our love. My friends and I decided "Tea Time" is a lovely way to celebrate each other's birthdays. Two years ago I was given a Birthday Tea Party. We had little sandwiches, cookies, little cakes, and pots and pots of hot tea. One lump or two?

The Tea Party

We'll have a Tea said she
A birthday Tea for me?
Oh yes, It will be quite divine
As you sip yours and
I sip mine!

The girlfriends visit, sip and eat
An afternoon Tea is such a treat

We shared our thoughts of heart and soul
We were not sad, we were not droll

But rather cherished friendship talk
of ways we live and
ways we walk

So here's to you and me
and the precious, precious
cup of tea
That we call friendship

The legacy of "I love you." Years ago, I knew a woman who had a very large family. Her children were always coming, going and telephoning. I was impressed by her expression of "I love you" every time they departed or when a phone call would end. I chose to emulate her love gift in my own family. Just a few minutes ago, Candy phoned me from her office, and she ended our conversation with, "I love you." Remember that the mother's heart is the child's classroom. How you love, your child will love. They're always watching . . .

Tuck love notes in your husband's briefcase or the children's lunches. My husband loved to make the girls' lunches and would include a quotation or Bible verse. This continued well into high school and even when Candy returned after college and began her career. Candy remarked, "Dad, when I open my brown bag, everyone asks, "What did your dad write today?" Love passed on to **many** hearts through a brown bag lunch!

Give the gift of sweet words to your sweetheart. In Solomon's Song of Songs 1:16 it says, "How handsome you are, my lover! Oh, how charming!" In 4:9 it goes on to say, "You have stolen my heart, my sister, my bride; you have stolen my heart." When was the last time you shared such **endearing** words with the one you love?

Show love by walking your husband, child, friend, relative, or visitor to the front door when they are leaving. Better yet, walk out with them to the car and **wave** good-bye.

Send travelers off with a prayer. Tuck a note in their suitcase with this verse on it:

May the Lord keep watch between you and me when we are away from each other.—Genesis 31:49

"**Romance in marriage**" is one of my most requested talks. Women love their husbands and want to create romantic times but are often SIDETRACKED by the everyday demands of life. Please know that I know husbands can sometimes be hard to love . . . but so can we! Let's be initiators and refresh our marriages with a reromanticizing exercise:

♥ Think of what first attracted you to your husband. Was it his smile, intellect, sense of humor? Remember?

♥ He loved you so much that he asked you to spend the rest of your life with him. "Will you marry me?" Remember?

♥ Keep a really good picture of your husband where you'll see it all the time and remember what you love most about your relationship.

XOXO

Express love to your husband uniquely. I surprised Tom the morning of our wedding anniversary and wrote "I love you!" on the bathroom mirror in lipstick. (It easily came off with glass cleaner.) He was so pleased, he took a picture!

I have given many greeting cards to my husband. But last Valentine's Day I wrote him this SPECIAL "love letter." With Tom's permission I have created copies for the women who hear my "Romance in marriage" message. Here's a copy for you.

For my Husband

In the beginning
I couldn't believe
I'd finally met you

The One

Dreaming of, praying for
and wondering about

The One

And suddenly there you were
Your smile, personality and heart
so irresistible

You became the focus of
my love and our future

Remembering brings such joy
because
I love you
and I love us together,
Tom and Dolley.
(you can insert your names here)

I so desire to keep our
love, friendship and marriage
fresh, new, playful, and fulfilling.

This is my commitment and Valentine
gift to you and to us.

Little Sweetheart Cakes

my family loves dessert, especially cake! and I like presenting a fresh cake for dessert, as opposed to a leftover one. I think it makes them feel more loved! So, I bake several smaller cakes from one box of cake mix. I frost one, freeze the rest, and store the remaining frosting in the refrigerator. This way I'm always prepared to serve a fresh cake or put one together as a gift. If you're really in a hurry you can microwave defrost the cake and soften the frosting. However, I usually just set both out on the kitchen counter for about a half-hour.

Prepare one box of white (or other flavor) cake mix according to the instructions on the box.

Spray several different sizes of cake pans with nonstick spray. I use two small- to medium-sized metal heart pans (6 1/4" and 8") and four little metal heart pans. If you have some vintage tin Jell-O molds they also work nicely for little cakes.

Fill each pan with the batter a little more than half the way.

Bake at 350 degrees for approximately 30 minutes for little cakes, or 40 to 45 minutes for the small- to medium-sized ones, or until a knife comes out clean when tested.

When done remove from oven and cool.

Remove cakes from pans, put one on a serving plate. Freeze the rest individually in freezer-zip-lock bags for future use.

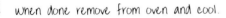

To Give as a Gift:

I like to take the little heart cakes and frost and coconut them the same way. But instead of putting them on a serving plate, I place them on colorful paper plates (a solid color is best), wrap them in cellophane and tie with a ribbon. you can also omit the paper plate and wrap with cello- phane only. This becomes a little, but thoughtful, gift to a teacher, office worker, neighbor, or whomever the Holy Spirit puts on your heart for some just lovin' desserts!

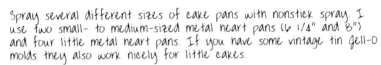

Buttercream Frosting

I make a full buttercream recipe then store the unused portion in the refrigerator for future use.

1 stick of butter	1 tbsp. vanilla (scant)
1 lb. powdered sugar	Fresh milk, low fat or whole

Cream the butter with an electric mixer. Add vanilla. Then add powdered sugar. (Mixture will be dry.) Slowly add milk and mix to desired consistency. Frost the cake that you have placed on the serving plate. Generously sprinkle with coconut.

Clean up around the edges and place a pretty ribbon bow on the plate above the cake. You can also surround the cake with lemon leaves or ferns from your garden (just make sure your guests don't eat them). Refrigerate decorated cake (because of the milk and butter in the frosting) until serving.

Voila!
Enjoy!
And God Bless!

The Heart of God Loves You and me

Always remember that there isn't anything you or I can do to get God to love us any more or any less. He just loves us! Jesus loves me this I know!

That best portion of a good man's life, His little, nameless, unremembered acts of kindness and of love.
—William Wordsworth

Forgiveness

and throughout all eternity I forgive you, you forgive me.—William Blake

Just as God forgives our sin through Christ, He wants us to pass the gift of forgiveness from His heart on to one another. Ephesians 4:32 advises us to "be kind and COMPASSIONATE to one another, forgiving each other, just as in Christ God forgave you." The really good news is that every day is new in Jesus! Every day we have the opportunity to drop grudges, forgive, ask to be forgiven, and begin anew. Do you have any relationships that are in need of mending?

There's no time like the present to consider what you can do to REACH OUT in love, forgive, ask to be forgiven, and RESTORE a relationship to peace and joy.

Then Peter came to Jesus and asked, "Lord, how many times shall I forgive my brother when he sins against me? Up to seven times?" Jesus answered, "I tell you, not seven times, but seventy-seven times."—Matthew 18:21-22

If you need to Forgive Someone
. . .the actual words, "I forgive you," may be too blunt. You could say, "I miss our friendship," followed by an invitation to meet soon. Be specific! "Tea on Tuesday at 2:00?" or "I'll call this weekend to see if that's a good time for you." Remember, if you aim at nothing, you'll hit it every time. Consider sending a written invitation. It offers the other person (and you too!) GRACE and space to think and pray.

If you Seek Forgiveness
. . .write a very personal letter of love, including the message, "Please forgive me." Don't include a lengthy explanation, just express love through HUMILITY.

Finally, all of you, live in harmony with one another; be sympathetic, love as brothers, be compassionate and humble.—1 Peter 3:8

Bridging the Gap
Send a simple greeting card with an expression of love and friendship. Depending on the situation, the perfect card to break the ice could be humorous or whimsical. Remember, "angels fly high, because they take things lightly."

A cheerful heart is good medicine—Proverbs 17:22

Keeping the Focus
When you ask someone to forgive you, keep it simple and focus on mending the relationship, not reliving part of the dispute. I once received a letter from a woman who apologized for hurting me, but went on (for two more pages!) to explain what I did to cause her to hurt me. I refer to this type of apology as the "However . . . ." clause.

Letting Go of Blame
At a retreat, a young woman came up to me after the morning message and asked for counsel. She and her friend had a serious falling out and hadn't spoken to each other for almost a year. The young woman missed her friend very much and was considering calling or writing her a letter of apology. She went on to say, "I plan to ask my friend to admit her wrongdoing and responsibility in our estrangement." I strongly encouraged her to decide what was more important: their friendship or having the last word! You can't have both and need to approach brokeness with the mending tools of grace and mercy. Blame keeps the wound open, forgiveness helps it to heal.

Fruits of Forgiveness

Galatians 5:22-23 reminds us that the fruit of the Spirit is "love, joy, peace, patience, kindness, goodness, faithfulness, gentleness, and self-control . . ." Here's how I apply them to forgiveness:

- LOVE her/him just as she/he is
- JOY through forgiveness
- PEACE at last!
- PATIENCE with her/his human nature
- KINDNESS in the mending of relationships
- GOODNESS from Jesus through you to her/him
- FAITHFULNESS to God's command to forgive and forgive and forgive
- GENTLENESS like the Lamb of God
- SELF-CONTROL to resist the "However" or "Last Word" clause

Peace Offerings

Gifts of favorite foods (this works especially well with boyfriends and husbands) or flowers can be a good peace offering. Accompany the gift with a little note saying something like "I was thinking of you and know how much you like chocolate chip cookies. Enjoy!" or "I saw these and remembered how much you enjoy sunflowers." This gesture demonstrates that you really do care, and can often bridge the gap between hurt and healing.

Clothe yourselves with compassion, kindness, humility, gentleness and patience. Bear with each other and forgive whatever grievances you may have against one another.—Colossians 3:12-13

A Really Good Chocolate Chip Cookie Recipe!

2/3 cup shortening (I combine 1/3 cup butter
and 1/3 cup shortening)
1/2 cup light brown sugar
1 egg
1 tsp. vanilla
1 1/2 cups flour
1/2 tsp. baking soda
1/2 tsp. salt
1/2 cup nuts (optional)
6 oz. chocolate chips

With an electric beater combine butter and shortening. Add brown sugar and mix. Add granulated sugar and mix. Then mix in egg and vanilla.

In a separate bowl, sift together flour, soda and salt. Gently add to the creamed mixture until blended. By hand, stir in the chocolate chips and nuts. Drop by generous teaspoonfuls on an ungreased cookie sheet. Bake in a preheated 375-degree oven for 8 to 12 minutes.

Makes 4 to 5 dozen small cookies.

Mercy

Be merciful, just as your Father is merciful. —Luke 6:36

 mercy isn't a deserved gift, it's a true "gift from the heart." mercy loves, comforts, pardons, and helps, just as the Savior loves, comforts, pardons, and helps His children. mercy is Jesus loving them through us, and Jesus loving us through them.

Ironically, the precious gift of mercy is one we love to receive but often find very expensive to give. Consider this: How often have you deeply longed for mercy? But the harder question is how many times have you freely given it? For most of us the painfully honest answer is that we haven't given the gift of mercy nearly enough.

mercy when your Heart Says "no Way!"

There will always be people in our lives who are less than kind. It's not easy to be merciful toward someone who is hurting you, and the desire to get even or ignore him or her is tempting. However, if you can remember that people who hurt are usually hurting, a merciful heart isn't very far away. Jesus will help you! Come with me, step into the light of His love, and say this little prayer: "Take me out, Jesus, and put You in." Because Jesus is the author of mercy, He will hear your prayer and lovingly write patience, mercy and understanding on to the ways of your heart.

Let us fix our eyes on Jesus, the author and Perfecter of our faith. —Hebrews 12:2

32

mercy for the Disadvantaged, Helpless and Poor

When we catch a glimpse of someone indigent, it's so easy to judge him or her. Thoughts run through our minds, "Get a job!" or "Why should I help you?" Quite often when I'm driving I will see someone at a freeway exit or entrance holding a sign asking for money or food. I won't give money in that circumstance, but I always have food (granola bars, cheese and pretzel packs, boxed drinks) to give. Food from Jesus, through me, to a lost lamb who needs mercy. Do you know of someone who could use mercy from you?

He who oppresses the poor shows contempt for their maker, but whoever is kind to the needy honors God.—Proverbs 14:31

mercy for Other Drivers

Here's an easy way to take your mercy "temperature": the next time you're driving consider how you "talk" to other drivers—in your thoughts, words, or gestures. mercy!

For the driver who cuts you off, or changes lanes without signaling, or is driving 20 miles below the speed limit . . . extend mercy! Remember, nobody's perfect! And, undoubtedly, some day it will be your turn.

Blessed are the merciful, for they will be shown mercy.—Matthew 5:7

merry Christmas mercy Received

It was the holiday season and while pulling out of a parking space, I hit another car. The damage was minor, but damage nonetheless. The lady who owned the car got out, looked at the damage and said, "It's not that bad, honey. Let's just forget it. merry Christmas!"

a merciful Heart of Second Chances

I had to repeat second grade, and at the beginning of the new school year I went to the third grade classroom hoping no one would remember. Someone did. And it wasn't long before Sister Catherine, the second grade teacher, came and collected me. My heart was pounding as we walked down the hall together. Sister Catherine warmly put her arm around me and said, "You're not in trouble, dear. Don't worry, we'll have a good year together." In second grade, the second time around, I turned the corner academically and excelled. mercy gives second chances!

I love the Lord, for He heard my voice; He heard my cry for mercy. Because He turned his ear to me, I will call on Him as long as I live.—Psalm 116:1-2

mercy for Those Overwhelmed

The next time you find yourself listening to a friend who has more on her list than time to do it, remember this:

Judgment would bark: "You have just as much time as I do. Why is it so difficult for you to get things done?"

Criticism would scream: "You need to stop procrastinating and manage your time better!"

mercy would gently say: "I'm coming to help you and, together, we'll get it done in no time."

This is what the Lord Almighty says: "Administer true justice; show mercy and compassion to one another."—Zechariah 7:9

*The heart that grants mercy
Doesn't keep credits and debts
Mercy grants pardon
Pardon forgives and forgets*

Comfort

As a mother comforts her child, so will I comfort you.—Isaiah 66:13

Comfort comes to you and me through the Comforter—the Holy Spirit. And it is through His guidance that we are inspired to reach out to others. This is God's family at work, heart-to-heart with the gift of comfort.

Comfort from a Helping Heart

Our spontaneous response to someone's loss or crisis is often a sincere, "If there's anything I can do, please let me know." Although our intention is good, it often falls short because people in crisis aren't usually able to think clearly enough to anticipate what they need. So instead of asking them, ask the Lord. See how He leads your heart, and then jump into action!

Comforters who Jumped into Action

My entire family was sick, including me, the mom! Dinnertime arrived, and I was trying desperately to think of something easy to prepare. Just then the doorbell rang. It was my friend Judy . . . bringing an entire meal for our family. Her explanation? "The Lord just told me to make an extra dinner for the Carlsons." Judy didn't know our situation, but the Lord did! And when He spoke to her heart she listened, and we were blessed and comforted!

When Grandpa died it was so sudden! We were all in shock as we planned the memorial service and tried to comfort Grandma and ourselves. There was no time for meal preparation, so we existed primarily on fast food. Ugh! In the midst of our sorrow and chaos, my friend Teri called and said, "I want to bring a pot roast dinner to your family. What night would you like me to deliver it?" Manna from heaven! We were so comforted by her generosity and good meal. Teri didn't ask how she could help, she just took action!

Comfort, comfort my people, says your God.
—Isaiah 40:1

35

Words of Comfort

Words of comfort need to be fresh expressions of love, concern and sympathy—not stale, overused phrases. It's so quick and easy to use familiar phrases, but please know that a greater blessing will come from thoughtfulness and prayer before giving a word of comfort.

I love you.

We/he/she love(s) you.

It's normal, she's just "individuating" (said of one of our daughters when she was a teenager acting like a teenager).

He's with the Lord now.

Would you like me to put your request on the prayer chain?

Dinner is ready!

Come for breakfast!

How's your mom/dad doing?

Call me anytime of day or night—I'm here.

I'll arrange everything.

It's just a season.

I promise with my whole heart that I will pray for you.

There's nothing that happens to you or me that the Lord doesn't know about.

"Everything's going to be okay!"

Let your conversation be always full of grace.
—Colossians 4:6

The family of God needs earthly angels who will fly from need to need with heavenly comfort. And that's my friend Teri! She loves people, and if a need arises, she's there. Here are just a few ways I've seen her heart give comfort:

For young men in ministry, about to be married, or between apartments, and in need of temporary housing, Teri and her husband have opened their home countless times.

For families in crisis, her loving words and promises of constant prayer have brought great comfort.

For the bereaved, infirm, or tired new mothers, she has graciously delivered homemade comfort food from her kitchen.

For an unwed mother, she opened her home and heart, comforting her through the pregnancy, delivery, and eventual adoption of the baby into a Christian family.

For you know that we dealt with each of you as a father deals with his own children, encouraging, comforting and urging you to live lives worthy of God.
—1 Thessalonians 2:11-12

Comforting in Everyday Ways

1. Offering a hot cup of tea or coffee
2. Making a telephone call
3. Sending a note of reassurance and love

Blankets of Comfort

By the time I was twenty-three, both of my parents were deceased. And, when Candy was born three years later, I missed having them be there to see their first grandchild. Although the Lord had given me the most wonderful in-laws, I was sad there weren't grandparents from my family.

And then the comfort came. An aunt I hadn't seen for several years (she lives in Boston, I in California) heard of the new baby and sent her a darling pink hand-crocheted blanket with a little note saying how pleased she was to be a grand aunt. The Lord sent comfort through Aunt Jane's loving heart.

I will not leave you as orphans; I will come to you.—John 14:18

Comfort with Pampering

Turn down the bed covers for your husband, child or houseguest. It will make him or her feel cared for and just a little pampered. But most of all, it's a comfort!

Comfort with Silence

In the quest to comfort and console, we frequently find ourselves searching for just the right words. Sometimes the right words are no words at all—"sounds of silence" as we show up and sit still with our friend or loved one.

38

For Those Who Lose a Loved One

Send flowers to their home rather than the funeral home.

Blessed are those who mourn, for they will be comforted.—Matthew 5:4

Send a fruit basket to the family's home, where everyone gathers. It will provide quick, healthy snacks and be a comforting reminder of your love.

They set out from their homes and met together by agreement to go and sympathize with him and comfort him. . . . No one said a word to him, because they saw how great his suffering was.—Job 2:11, 13

Send a letter of comfort. When my husband's father went home to be with the Lord, many people wrote letters of what they appreciated about Dad or how he had ministered to them. It takes a little more time to write a letter but, oh, how we were comforted by them!

So the Lord spoke kind and comforting words to the angel who talked with me.—Zechariah 1:13

Step in to help meet the practical needs. Although this is a very difficult and emotional task, sorting through possessions and freshening a room or two for the deceased's family is a true gift from the heart. The Lord usually leads the brother or sister with a servant's heart to this need and gives him or her supernatural ability to see it through to completion.

Comfort Foods

a grilled cheese sandwich and a chocolate milkshake
Cream of wheat
meatloaf with mashed potatoes, baby peas and applesauce

a chocolate milkshake (worth mentioning twice)
Vanilla ice cream
Hot tea and buttered toast

a peanut butter sandwich and a tall glass of milk

Did I mention a chocolate milkshake?
(actually, chocolate anything will do!)

an old-fashioned pot roast dinner

apple pie à la mode
Homemade custard

Be comforted, dear friend, and enjoy!

Praise be to the God and Father of our Lord Jesus Christ, the Father of compassion and the God of all comfort, who comforts us in all our troubles, so that we can comfort those in any trouble with the comfort we ourselves have received from God.—2 Corinthians 1:3-4

 # Celebration

Be joyful always.—1 Thessalonians 5:16

Just Celebrate!

Whether it's for your children, neighbors, parents, grandparents, friends, boss, secretary, or whomever, take the **time** to rejoice and celebrate! It's easy to say, "Oh, maybe next time," or "next year," or "I'm just not up to it right now." The opportunity may never come again.

Keep it simple

and

celebrate today!

What makes a celebration? Quite often it's balloons, good food, great desserts, and the element of **surprise**. But more important elements are the "gifts from the heart" of love, generosity, enthusiasm, dedication, and, most of all, sacrifice and selflessness. After all, putting together any type of celebration, whether large or small, takes effort and expense. Don't know where to begin? Here are some ideas to help you get started!

Celebrate the New Day

Pack a simple breakfast picnic and "kidnap" (the element of surprise adds to the celebration!) your friend, husband, children, or parents and watch the sunrise. Declare **praise** and thanksgiving to the Lord as you admire the beauty of His creation!

I have come into the world as a light, so that no one who believes in Me should stay in darkness.—John 12:46

Celebrate the Bride-to-Be

Traditionally, we honor the bride with a "shower" of tangible gifts, but we can also give her a "gift from the heart" by taking the time to have each married woman share advice she was given as a bride or "wifely wisdom" from experience. One lady spoke of the special request her mother made minutes before the wedding ceremony: "Honey, please don't tell me of your quarrels, because long after you've forgiven your husband, I will remember!" How true!

Celebrate the New Baby

When Doug and Karen hosted a couples' shower for their neighbors' baby girl, they began a heartening tradition centered around a "gift from the heart." As each couple held baby Rachel, they said a prayer of love and dedication, then gently placed her in the arms of the next couple in this circle of celebration and support. What a wonderful way for a precious bundle from heaven to begin life!

Celebrate the New Grandmother

Grandma needs almost as much baby equipment at her house as the new mother. Share her joy by celebrating with a "Grandbaby Shower." In the invitation ask each guest to include a little note with her gift, telling how she was especially blessed by her own grandmother. (For example, words of wisdom, practical instruction, or love expressed in any number of ways.) Include a pretty piece of stationery with the invitation, then place these "gifts from the heart" in a pretty album for the grandmother's delight and inspiration!

Celebrate Sweet 16

This is such a pivotal age for a young girl. My husband, Tom, and I were inspired to give each of our girls a "rite of passage" party after attending the bat mitzvah of one of Candy's friends. Our invitation read:

Sweet 16

With grateful hearts
for our family and friends
who have been such an important influence
in our daughter's life,
we invite you to join us for . . .

Katie's Sweet Sixteen

Afternoon Tea—Open House
Sunday, August 28, 1994
Two o'clock to Four-Thirty

RSVP
Tom & Dolley Carlson

Also included on a separate enclosure:
"Your friendship is Katie's greatest gift. no other gifts please. would you be so kind as to write her a letter of 'I remember when' or a good wish for the future on the enclosed stationery? It will be placed in an album she will have forever as a remembrance of the caring and loving people God has brought into her life."

Celebration Party Apparel

Several years ago, my father-in-law bought matching "party shirts" for each male in our family. The party attire never ceased to bring joy and **laughter** to each family event. This inspired us to create matching baseball caps (with "Happy 80th" written on them in puff fabric paint) for Grandpa's birthday. After the party, Grandma collected the caps and now **loans** them out to her friends for other eightieth birthday celebrations!

Celebrate the First Day of School

Have an at-home pizza party, let the answering machine take your calls and **completely** dedicate the evening to hearing all about the new teacher, "Guess who's in my class?" and so on. It will communicate to your children the importance of their education, your interest in them and will make this time of year **extra special**—and fun, too!

Celebrate Your Marriage

Don't wait for your wedding anniversary. Arrange for a babysitter and surprise your husband on a week night (when he'll **least** expect it) with his favorite dinner. Have a beautifully set table in front of the fireplace, or eat in the backyard on a picnic blanket—by votive candlelight. Rent a romantic video (old movies are fabulous!) for after dinner. Some old movie ideas include "Roman Holiday" (1953) with Audrey Hepburn and Gregory Peck, "An Affair to Remember" (1957) with Deborah Kerr and Cary Grant, and, of course, "Casablanca" (1942) with Ingrid Bergman and Humphrey Bogart.

Celebration is not to be self-centered. Ezra connected celebration with giving. This gave those in need an opportunity as well. Often when we celebrate and give to others (even when we don't feel like it), we are strengthened spiritually and filled with joy. Enter into celebrations that honor God, and allow him to fill you with this joy.
—Footnote for Nehemiah 8:9-10 in the Life Application NIV Bible.

44

Heavenly Cream Dessert

This molded cream dessert is so easy and has been a favorite "celebration" dessert of my family and friends for many years.

1 cup + 3 tbsp. whipping cream
1/2 cup sugar
1 envelope plain gelatin
3/4 pint sour cream
1 tsp. vanilla

Mix the cream, sugar and gelatin in a saucepan and heat gently until the gelatin is thoroughly dissolved. Cool until slightly thickened. On low setting, beat in the sour cream and flavor with vanilla. Beat gently until smooth.

Lightly spray 3-cup metal mold or serving bowl with nonstick spray and add mixture. If you want to make individual servings, pour the cream into small individual molds. Cover and chill until set, at least 4 hours. I prefer to make this dessert the day before or morning of the celebration.

To unmold, quickly dip the container in hot water until the edges just begin to come loose (you may also go around the edges with a paring knife to help loosen the dessert). Invert the mold onto a serving plate and surround generously with sliced fresh strawberries and garnish with whole berries. Or serve defrosted frozen sliced strawberries on the side, in a bowl with a ladle.

I usually make this dessert in a heart mold and garnish the middle of the heart with one whole fresh strawberry (slice a little piece off the back so it will lie flat). You can also put a little fern and baby's breath or blue statice flowers here and there around the edge of the serving plate.

Enjoy!

Honor

Be devoted to one another in brotherly love. Honor one another above yourselves.—Romans 12:10

In today's society, often the most honored people have great intelligence, position or wealth—and sometimes all three! It's important for us to remember that the Lord's concern is with the richness or poverty of our heart's intent. And, it is our heart's good intent that makes us honorable. 1 Samuel 16:7 reminds us, "But the Lord looks at the heart."

Honor with Humility

Mother Teresa honors the Lord by loving, caring for and nursing the neediest of the needy—the downtrodden, the diseased and the dying. Mother Teresa's humble heart is rich with love, grace and selflessness.

He who oppresses the poor shows contempt for their maker, but whoever is kind to the needy honors God.—Proverbs 14:31

Honoring with Generosity

There was a woman in a local Bible study class whose father was dying. She wanted so much to see him one last time, but felt it was impossible because he lived overseas and she didn't have the financial resources for the trip. The Holy Spirit quickly moved in the hearts of the women in the class and everyone contributed to the airfare. Best of all, the presentation was made in a very quiet and private way. Sometimes we need to hear love shout and other times all we need is a whisper. The women in the Bible study were sensitive to this and I'm sure the Lord was well pleased.

In thy face I see the map of honor, truth, and loyalty.
—William Shakespeare

Honoring Grandpa

Grandpa loved to make things for the family. Our homes are filled with his wonderful creations: tables, charming little pine cabinets, coach benches with hidden storage space beneath the hinged seats, reindeer, angel candle holders, and a baby chair. We honored Grandpa's generosity on his birthday one year. All of his wonderful creations were put on display in the backyard with colorful signs stating: GRANDPA MADE THIS! He was thrilled and a little teary.

Honor your mother and father.—Mark 7:10

Honoring Toasts

Grandma hasn't been well and made a courageous effort to be with the family last Thanksgiving. We were so grateful for her presence and honored her in a very special way. The family toasted with glasses of sparkling apple cider: "Here's to the best mother-in-law in the world." "The best mother, too!" "Grandma is always praying for all of us. Thanks, Grandma!" "HEAR-HEAR!"

You can toast anytime . . . . even at regular weekday meals. "Here's to Bobby for doing so well on his spelling test!" "And here's to Chris for making her bed neatly two weeks in a row!" Also try this when you have another family over for dinner. Children love to toast, and you'll find it will create a joyous and honorable memory for all.

Her children arise and call her blessed; her husband also,
and he praises her.—Proverbs 31:28

Honoring with Video

Compiling a "This Is Your Life" video is a perfect way to commemorate and honor someone on his or her birthday, special occasion, graduation, anniversary, or retirement. We did this for Grandpa on his eightieth birthday. For weeks my husband and I viewed old family movies (some dating back to 1940), selecting excerpts for Grandpa's video. Double blessings were ours as we watched our father's **honorable** and **godly life** unfold night after night!

My honor is dearer to me than my life.—Cervantes

Honoring the Bride

If you're the maid of honor, you've been given a very special role. Honor the bride with your patience, loyalty and support. She's bound to get a little edgy, impatient and frustrated while finalizing all the details that go into planning a wedding. That's where you come in—just **love** her through it and be available to listen, listen, listen—and help!

Honoring Wedding Vows

I recently read the vows my husband and I recited on our wedding day, February 8, 1969. "Wilt thou have this man to be thy husband, and wilt thou pledge thy troth to him, in all love and honor, in all duty and service, in all faith and tenderness, to live with him, and cherish him, according to the ordinance of God, in the holy bond of marriage? The woman shall answer: I will."

How **blessed** you will be if you honor your vows, honor your husband, and honor your marriage.

Her husband has full confidence in her and lacks nothing of value. She brings him good, not harm, all the days of her life.
—Proverbs 31:11-12

Prayer

Prayer is a quiet, peaceful, and blessed place where we can seek the will of God as we praise, confess to, thank, and petition Him.

A Prayer . . . Heaven Sent!

This is a prayer that the Holy Spirit sent to me for my speaking ministry. It has since spilled over into every day of my life:

> Take me out, Jesus . . .
> and put You in . . .

When I submit to the will of Jesus, and act in a way that glorifies Him, life just goes better!

Start Your Day Off Prayerfully!

In the peacefulness of morning, when you first wake and before you rise, thank the Lord for your life and another day. Then begin praying, from the tip of your toes to the top of your head, the following prayer:

Lord, please guide my footsteps today, and let me be a blessing everywhere you take me.
Lord, please keep my body healthy.
Lord, please help me to have a loving, caring, and peaceful heart.
Lord, please keep my words tender and sweet, as someday I may need to eat them.
Lord, allow me to hear what You intend, and be deaf to lies, unkindness and evil.
Lord, allow my eyes to see needs, hurt and cares, and to capture the beauty of Your creation.
Lord, I submit my will to Yours. Thank You for hearing my morning prayer.
In Jesus' name, amen!

In the morning, O Lord, you hear my voice; in the morning I lay my requests before you and wait in expectation.—Psalm 5:3

49

Recipe for an Old-Fash

♥ Invite your sisters in Christ to gather together.

♥ Carefully plan the prayer time, including the opening and closing.

🍵 Remember to have a well-lit room (not bright but good light).

♥ A pretty, fragrant candle on the coffee table adds to the atmosphere.

♥ Turn down the volume on your answering machine and the ringer on your phone, unless you're expecting an important call. Loud ringing, recording and talking can quickly distract from the holiness of the moment.

♥ Select some of your favorite Christian tapes or CDs to softly play in the background. Music reaches our souls like nothing else and can help prepare hearts for prayer.

♥ Once you begin, it is essential that you stay on schedule.

♥ At the conclusion of prayer, have the group stand and hold hands. As the leader, thank the Lord for this circle of love and support. Send them off with His richest blessings and your gratitude for their loving hearts.

oned Prayer meeting

For a lunch-hour prayer meeting,
request that everyone bring a sack lunch. As the hostess, provide beverages and dessert.

Remain in me, and I will remain in you.—John 15:4

For an evening prayer meeting, have
a baked potato bar. Request that each person bring an ingredient such as grated cheese, sour cream, chives, bacon bits, chili, butter, fresh vegetables cut in small pieces (broccoli, carrots, mushrooms), and salsa. As the hostess, provide beverages and potatoes. Ask the dessert cook of your group to bring her best confectionery creation. The promise of chocolate can often provide the perfect incentive for ladies to leave their homes for an evening!

For where two or three come together in my name, there am I with them.
—Matthew 18:20

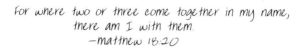

A day hemmed in prayer is less likely to unravel.

Friend-to-Friend Mug Exchange

Exchange a pretty mug with a friend, and pledge to pray for each other every time you use it. One woman told me she has never prayed so much for any one person in all her life. Her gift mug was especially cute, and she used it all the time, praying as she loaded it in the dishwasher, got it out of the dishwasher, put it in the cabinet, got it out of the cabinet, and when she used it!

The Great Gossip Stopper!

Stop gossip in its tracks with the power of prayer. Gently stop a friend from continuing with a story she shouldn't be telling by saying, "I understand. Let's stop and pray for her right now."

Prayer Reminders

My daughters and I have the same Irish Claddagh ring. Every time I notice my ring, I pray for the girls. I'm also reminded to pray for my husband every time I look at my wedding ring. (And I still get butterflies when I notice the engagement ring and remember the very special young man who asked me to be his wife!)

A Basketful of Prayer Requests

Overwhelmed by all the people you have promised to pray for? Take all your requests before the Lord, praying a general prayer. Then pick one to focus on for the day. It's like reaching into a basketful of prayer requests and pulling out one that needs extra and immediate attention.

Rejoice

Shout with joy to God, all the earth!—Psalm 66:1

Rejoice Along Life's Way

My friend Anne loves to rejoice! Her love for those of us who call her friend is boundless. The verse "He will yet fill your mouth with laughter and your lips with shouts of joy" (Job 8:21) is fulfilled in her walk with Him. She hasn't been without sorrow, but her hope is in the Lord. And she has always bounced back—rejoicing! Some ways I have seen her rejoice for others are:

- ♥ Sending flowers to an away-from-home college girl on her 21st birthday.

- ♥ Planning countless birthday dinners, luncheons and breakfasts.

- ♥ Hosting block parties on special holidays, such as Fourth of July and Christmas.

- ♥ Rejoicing in the writing of this book.

Rejoice, dear sisters, rejoice in the Lord. Oh, how He loves you and me!

Rejoice in the Beauty of God's Creation

My husband, Tom, and I love the outdoors. We enjoy hiking, especially in the Sierra Nevada mountains where we can shout to our hearts' content, "Thank You, Lord!"

The four seasons proclaim His creative hand:
Winter shouts with masses of snow and bare trees
silhouetted against earth and sky.
Spring shouts with new sprouts of
flowers, fruit and fauna.
Summer shouts with longer days that we
may gaze upon creation just a little longer.
Fall shouts with crimson leaves and golden rich harvests.
Rejoice in all His creation!

Rejoice in Jesus' Gift

There will be times when you won't feel like rejoicing. Times when all you want or need is a place of refuge. Jesus knows this and has provided a place for all His children to feel comforted and loved—His Word. By reading the Bible, you will find your way back to joy. When your heart is filled with joy, you'll have so much more to give to others.

Rejoice in Random Gifts

I am so blessed by others when they openly rejoice in the Lord. "God is so good." "Praise God!" "The Lord went before us and . . ." Our free and uninhibited acknowledgment of the Lord in public may serve as a random introduction to someone who doesn't know Him. What a priceless and, perhaps, eternal gift! Please remember to express your joy sincerely and not by design.

Rejoice with Music

When we rejoice in the Lord with music, it ministers to our hearts and souls like nothing else, filling us with His love and joy. And out of this fullness we are better able to keep on giving and giving. One of my favorite ways to listen to praise music is while power walking on Balboa Island. I pop a praise tape in my Walkman® and go—rejoicing in the Lord, rejoicing in the day, rejoicing in praise!

Sing to the Lord a new song, sing to the Lord, all the earth.—Psalm 96:1

Rejoice with the Bride- and Groom-to-Be

Tom and I are at an age when many of our friends' children are getting married. One of the ways we love to support and rejoice with these families is with "Wedding Soup." The week before a wedding is usually quite hectic with out-of-town family and friends arriving, rehearsals, last-minute details, and so on. I love to bring the bride or groom's family a "wedding soup" gift from the heart. This provides some relief from meal planning because a pot of hot soup is always on the stove. I accompany it with baguettes from the bakery, grated parmesan cheese, and a simple dessert such as Fudge-Topped Brownies (see Affirmation chapter)!

*Rejoice with me and I with thee
That Jesus loves us all!*

WEDDING SOUP
(Chicken Vegetable Soup)

For the broth:

3 1/2 lb. stewing chicken   1/2 onion, chopped
salt & pepper (to taste)   2 stalks of celery, cut in thirds
one carrot, cut in thirds

Empty chicken of gizzard and liver packet. Rinse chicken inside and out with cold
water. Place chicken in a large kettle and cover with cold water. Add carrot, celery, onion, salt and pepper. Bring to a boil, then turn down to low and simmer
for 1 1/2 hours.

Remove chicken and cool slightly. Pour broth through strainer (discard carrot, celery and onion) into large bowl and then back into large kettle. Cover and refrigerate for several hours or overnight so the fat will rise to the top. Remove fat.
Remove skin from chicken, then remove chicken from bones. Cut chicken into
nickle-sized pieces. Reserve to add to soup at end of cooking time.

For the vegetables:

8 medium carrots, cut lengthwise and sliced
8 stalks of celery, cut lengthwise and sliced
1 onion, chopped
8 zucchini, cut lengthwise and sliced
8 mushrooms, sliced (optional)
1 16 oz. bag frozen corn kernels
1 lb. 12 oz. can of crushed tomatoes (including liquid)

Add to chicken broth and bring to a boil. Immediately reduce heat and
simmer on low for one hour. Add chopped chicken last 15 minutes. Season
with marjoram, salt and pepper to taste OR eliminate the marjoram and
add fresh salsa to taste (the last 10 minutes). Also, a little grated
parmesan cheese sprinkled on each bowl of soup is delicious!

Tradition

The word "tradition" is almost synonymous with the musical "Fiddler on the Roof." The main character, Tevye, sings in a powerful voice with great passion and conviction the words "Tradition! Tradition!" He exclaims, "How do we keep our balance? That I can tell you in one word, TRADITION!"

Tradition is a gift of legacy from the heart. It offers us and our children a constant we can look forward to and depend on. How comforting it is to hear someone declare, "See you same time, same place, next year!" Traditions within a family offer children a secure place to observe, learn and then pass on the same customs to the next generation. I always associate the phrase "This is our tradition" with a sense of well-being and belonging. And if I'm not part of that tradition, very often my heart will long to participate!

One-on-One Time

For my daughters and me, our one-on-one time became an after-school tradition since the first day candy returned from kindergarten. In the "olden days," before answering machines, I would take the phone off the hook after school. We would then enjoy chips, salsa, Pepsi©, and lots of conversation. Sometimes the girls don't want to talk, so we just sit and snack together. It's our time and I have protected it as our tradition. Last year Katie graduated from high school. During the first week of summer she asked me if we could still have our three o'clock time. This year she's away at college, but when she's home we still have our afternoon time. It has provided a wonderful catalyst for conversation between mother and daughters.

The Written Blessing

I asked my parents for a very special devotional for my 10th birthday. It had gold-edged pages and a leather cover. I was so happy when my parents presented it to me. My mother wrote these words on the inside cover:

Dear Ruth Ann,

May you open this book often, as a guide to your daily living.

Love, Mummy & Daddy

The year was 1955. Eight years later my mother died. Long ago I lost the devotional but not the inspirational words my mother wrote. They are INSCRIBED on my heart forever. To this day, I have never given my daughters a book without writing a meaningful inscription in it.

Here's a copy of a special greeting that was sent to my husband for his first birthday by the Sunday School superintendent of North Park Church, Mabel Carlson, June 6, 1944:

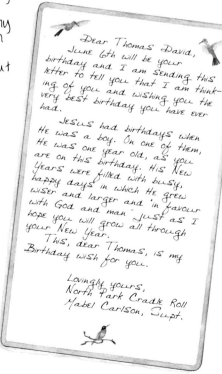

Dear Thomas David,

June 6th will be your birthday and I am sending this letter to tell you that I am thinking of you and wishing you the very best birthday you have ever had.

Jesus had birthdays when He was a boy. On one of them, He was one year old, as you are on this birthday. His New Years were filled with busy, happy days in which He grew wiser and larger and "in favour with God and man." Just as I hope you will grow all through your New Year.

This, dear Thomas, is my Birthday wish for you.

Lovingly yours,
North Park Cradle Roll
Mabel Carlson, Supt.

A Christian Heritage

The gift of faith can be imparted to your
children as you continue or establish the
tradition of Christian teaching in your
home. My husband had the blessing of
having two sets of grandparents who were Christians.
The depth of his faith is reflective of generations
of Christian tradition.

In his heart a man plans his course, but the Lord determines
his steps.—Proverbs 16:9

God is love

When Tom and I were first married, my mother-in-law
gave me a large envelope with the words Tommy's
Precious Papers. Many of them are Sunday School
certificates, records and handicrafts. My very favorite is
a little construction paper tulip with "God
is Love" handprinted on the stem. Tom
made this as a very little boy.

Currently he teaches Sunday School,
and a little boy in his class made a
construction paper cross with three
crayon-drawn hearts across the middle. Tom
asked what the hearts represented, and Cameron
replied, "God is love." The tradition of Christian teaching
continues from Chicago in 1946 to Newport Beach
in 1996.

But as for you, continue in what you have learned and have become convinced
of, because you know those from whom you learned it, and now from infancy
you have known the holy Scriptures, which are able to make you wise
for salvation through faith in Christ Jesus.—2 Timothy 3:14

Irish Greetings

When I was growing up, the gift from the heart tradition in my family and extended family was to kiss each other on the cheek and say, "Good-bye and God bless you," or "Good night and God bless you." My Uncle Johnny lives in Boston and after having a wonderful telephone conversation with him recently, Uncle Johnny said, "Good night and God bless you, hon." This tradition has its ORIGINS in Ireland where people enter a home with "God bless this house and all who are in it," and greet strangers on the way to work with, "God bless the work." And God bless you, dear reader!

As you enter the home, give it your greeting.—Matthew 10:12

Anticipated Arrivals

Another tradition in our family is to prepare and freshen the house in anticipation of the return of a family member after being away from home. When our young daughters returned from camp, there would always be at least one change or new decoration in their bedroom. This tradition began when I was a child and went away to summer camp on Cape Cod with my brother Bob. We knew our parents would "prepare" our rooms while we were gone, and upon our return home we felt so loved and special. Just imagine the way you and I will feel when we get to heaven and Jesus takes us to the room He has prepared for us in His Father's house! In the musical, "My Fair Lady," Eliza Doolittle sang, "All I want is a room somewhere." How about heaven, Eliza?

In my Father's house are many rooms. . . . I am going there to prepare a place for you.—John 14:2

60

Carlson Christmas
Holiday Traditions

Ethnic traditions are especially meaningful to us during the holidays. My husband is Swedish, while my family is Irish and English. On Christmas Eve, we have the tradition of the Swedish smorgasbord: ham, Swedish meatballs, pickled herring, potato sausage, limpa bread, lingonberries, and rice pudding. Heaven! Each family contributes something to the dinner and we take turns hosting.

Also on Christmas Eve, the Irish tradition of putting a single candle (battery operated for safety) in a window is continued in our home. The candle indicates there is ROOM in your home and heart for the Baby Jesus. My grandmother, Nora Catherine Foley, immigrated to America from County Galway, Ireland, at the turn of the century and brought with her this precious Christmas tradition from the heart.

On Christmas morning we play "The Messiah" music. And Tom prepares Swedish pancakes for the family's breakfast. I'm not quite sure how the tradition of Tom cooking them came to be, but I don't question it! I've included the pancake recipe, but you'll have to find the cook.

Another exciting English tradition is that of "crackers" at a party or holiday meal. Crackers are party favors made out of paper, filled with little token gifts and (this is the best part) a colorful tissue hat! To open the cracker you pull on two little tabs and a loud snap or crack is produced. We've worn these festive hats at many a Christmas dinner. It's so much fun!

HAPPY BIRTHDAY, JESUS!

Our family also celebrates the Savior's birth by serving a birthday cake for Jesus at Christmas dinner. In truth what began as an elaborate, home-made cake has evolved into a Christmas cake roll from an ice cream store! We order chocolate cake, vanilla ice cream and white icing. They decorate it with little holly leaves and berries and also provide candles. Happy Birthday, Jesus!

Throughout the years, our family has had the tradition of celebrating Christmas dinner with five other couples that we have been friends with for more than twenty years. Two couples host the dinner. They decide on a menu theme and are responsible for the main dish and an inexpensive but lovely table favor/gift for each couple to take home as a remembrance of the evening. They communicate the menu theme to the other couples, who then each bring the beverages, appetizers, salad, or dessert. We also have a "question of the evening" that unites us in one conversation around the dinner table. Last year the question was, "Where were you in 1962?" The answers were hilarious! We got to know each other even better as we shared laughter, a wonderful dinner, memories of '62, and, most of all, our love for each other!

What is important to you and your family? Pray about meaningful traditions, make a plan and make it happen! Traditions founded in Christianity can become eternal legacies for generations to come. One place to start is to support traditional ceremonies and passages. As my friend Dr. Stephanie McClellan says, "Never miss a wedding. Never miss a funeral."

Tom's Christmas morning Swedish Pancake Recipe

1 cup all-purpose flour

2 tbsp. sugar

1/4 tsp. salt

3 eggs

2 cups whole milk

2 tbsp. melted butter

Sift flour into bowl, then add sugar and salt. In a small bowl, beat the eggs. Stir eggs into the flour mixture. Gradually add the milk and stir until smooth. Add butter.

Heat griddle. Spread a small amount of vegetable oil or butter on the griddle as needed. With a large serving spoon pour batter onto griddle. Pancakes should be approximately 3" to 4" across. Fry on both sides until golden brown.

Place on warm platter in the oven. Serve with lingonberries and whipped cream or maple syrup and butter. Serves four.

God Jul!
(Swedish for Good Christmas!)

"Pass It On"

It only takes a spark to get a fire going,
and soon all those around
can warm up to its glowing
That's how it is with God's love
Once you experience it
You spread His love to everyone
You want to pass it on.

—Kurt Kaiser

What "spark" do others see in your life that warms them with the love of God? Friendship, affirmation, love, forgiveness, hope, mercy, comfort, honor, celebration, prayer, rejoicing, and tradition are all sparks. They're the true "gifts from the heart." They won't break your budget, but they will keep on giving and giving, from here to eternity!